Cross

We Suffer with Jesus

The Lutheran Spirituality Series

Holger Sonntag

CONCORDIA PUBLISHING HOUSE · SAINT LOUIS

Contents

> **Hymnal Key**
> *LSB=Lutheran Service Book*
> *ELH=Evangelical Lutheran Hymnary*
> *CW=Christian Worship*
> *LW=Lutheran Worship*
> *LBW=Lutheran Book of Worship*
> *TLH=The Lutheran Hymnal*

About This Series

In the West, spirituality is as nebulous as it is popular. Having succumbed to humanism, rationalism, and Darwinism, communities once known for a genuine Christian piety now provide a fertile breeding ground for self-made theologies, Eastern religions, the worship of science and technology, or even a resuscitation of the old pagan gods. In a highly competitive environment, each of these spiritual philosophies seeks to fill the vacuum left by the seemingly departed Christian spirit.

Even among faithful Christians, and at other times and places, spirituality has run the gamut from the mystical to the almost sterile. From the emotional to the pragmatic, the experiential to the cerebral, the all-too-human desire to experience (and control!) the divine has proven to be especially resilient. Influenced by modernism, postmodernism, and whatever comes next, even those who try faithfully to follow Jesus Christ may find defining *spirituality*, or at least what is distinctively Christian about their own beliefs and practices, a significant challenge.

Do Lutheran Christians have a spirituality? Indeed they do! This adult Bible study series explores the rich depths of a distinctively Lutheran spirituality that begins in Baptism and is founded upon God's Word. There, the incarnate, crucified, and resurrected Lord proclaims His victory over sin, death, and the devil, and from there flows the proclamation of His Gospel and the administration of His Sacraments. It is through these means presented within the liturgy of His Church that Christ communicates not merely spiritual energies, an emotional high, a method of reasoning, or a stringent morality, but truly Himself—God in human flesh.

Written by respected Lutheran scholars in the United States and Australia, this adult Bible study series emphasizes the Bible, Luther's catechism, and the Lutheran hymnal as concrete and integral resources for a truly Lutheran spirituality. May God richly bless those who study His Word, and through His Word may they experience the genuinely enlightening and life-giving spirituality found only in the life, death, and resurrection of our Lord and Savior, Jesus Christ.

The Editor

Participant Introduction

Martin Luther once identified three things that make a good theologian: *prayer* for the Holy Spirit to understand God's unique biblical Word; *meditation* on this Word; and, as the "touchstone," enduring *afflictions* due to meditating on God's Word. In this study, we'll unpack what Scripture has to say about afflictions in the life of the Christian, that is, the cross we will endure in various shapes and sizes, not *even though*, but *because* we are Christians.

Luther noticed a discrepancy in his day: On the one hand, Scripture is filled with passages about the necessary suffering of the saints in the world as they follow their crucified Lord in their concrete daily vocations in church, home, work, and state. On the other hand, the teaching and practice of many seemed to be about avoiding this God-sent cross at all costs. There were those who paid significant sums of money to avoid suffering in purgatory or to avoid the rather demanding forms of repentance. There were others who subjected themselves to a rigorous discipline of prayer, fasting, chastity, and poverty apart from any vocational discipleship in the biblical sense. In each and every case, Luther found, self-chosen, controlled forms of "suffering" were anxiously sought as spiritual paths—only to get around the "real deal" sent by God in His way and at His time. Distrusting God, breaking the First Commandment, is also at the bottom of this deformation.

Clearly, a reformation, a return to Scripture also in this area of spirituality, had become necessary. By the time the Diet of Augsburg occurred in 1530, Lutherans humbly confessed that in their churches people were well instructed from God's Word concerning the cross in the life and vocation of the Christian.

And today? Is Christianity promoted as a way to avoid "bad stuff" and to achieve worldly success? Or is Christianity taught as a life under the cross? Popular titles like 2004's *Your Best Life Now* by Joel Osteen suggest the former. Being "religious" is widely seen as a path to freedom from pain and failure. Suffering is seen as but an invigorating "challenge" on the road to reaching one's "full potential." "Spiritual disciplines" are observed, often at the expense of our God-given vocations and their trials, to achieve personal fulfillment, even salvation.

Lutherans faithful to God's Word have held out a different vision of Christianity and spirituality, one that is shaped by the cross of Christ and daily flows from Baptism. We now enter this unique and life-giving world of biblical Christianity.

To prepare for "Cross Meets Man: Baptism," read Romans 6:1–18.

C03

Cross Meets Man: Baptism

Who can blot out the Cross, which th' instrument
Of God, dewed on me in the Sacrament?

—John Donne, *The Cross*

Christians are reborn through the Word-filled waters of Baptism. We are marked with Christ's cross forever. Our lives are connected to the cross from the beginning. The cross is not accidental to the life of the Christian. Through Baptism, Christ's suffering and death on the cross gives us new life. It also teaches us how to lead this eternal life in time as we serve God and our neighbor in our vocations in church, home, work, and state—as pastors and parishioners; as husbands and wives; as parents and children; as employers and employees; as rulers and citizens.

1. What is the meaning and significance of Baptism in the life of a Christian? In your life?

Baptism and the Cross

2. Read Romans 6:1. What is the question Paul sets out to answer in this chapter?

3. Read Romans 6:3–8. How does Baptism answer question two above? In other words, why does Romans 6:2 give a negative answer to this question?

4. Read Romans 6:6; and Galatians 2:20; 5:24. How did this crucifying of the old Adam happen to us in Baptism?

5. Read Romans 6:4, 9–18; 8:13; and Colossians 3:5–17 (3:18–4:2!). How and where does the ongoing "crucifixion" in the post-Baptismal life of the Christian take place?

6. How is the new life of the Christian related to the Ten Commandments on the one hand and his or her post-resurrection life on the other hand?

7. Read Romans 7:15–23; and Galatians 5:17. Why is the life of the baptized a spiritual battle, with all the hardships of military service? In other words, why is it an ongoing "cross" of the Christian? How does a clear understanding of the power of sin in the life of the Christian make the means of grace more valuable?

A Closer Look at Baptism

In Baptism, God forgives all our sins for Christ's sake and gives us spiritual rebirth through God's Word and Spirit. However, we remain sinners who continue to sin. Quite apart from any other suffering we may or may not to have to endure as Christians, this struggle with its persistent failures is assured. These failures will in time come to make you wonder: "After all these years of unsuccessfully fighting my sinful nature, what does God think about me? Is He still graciously disposed toward me despite my failure?"

Baptism's promise declares: "Yes, for Christ's sake, God is still gracious to you, in spite of all your sins." This promise is spoken anew in the Divine Service at church, when the called and ordained pastor, in Christ's stead and by His command, forgives you all your sins. We also recall God's promises made to us in our Baptism when we read, hear, or remember Bible passages that refer to this Sacrament.

8. Read Titus 3:4–7. As Christ's baptized siblings, we strive to lead holy lives in the power of the Holy Spirit. Is it then holy living, "doing as well as we can," that saves us in the end? Does moral improvement offer any lasting comfort?

9. Baptism itself is embattled. Many churches misunderstand what Baptism is, does, and means. Some say it is a mere sign of our faith; others teach that it removes sin once but has no further relevance. Under the cross, how is the biblical teaching on Baptism both more realistic and comforting than other views?

Anti-Antinomianism

In the last decade of his earthly life, Luther battled the notion that, since Christians are redeemed by Christ alone, they need not engage sin in any serious way. Those holding this view were called "Antinomians" because they believed that God's Law, the Ten Commandments, no longer had a place among believers. Christians, they taught, had no need for their sins to be pointed out to them or to be encouraged to struggle daily against this sin in them; the proclamation of the Gospel was all that was needed.

Time and again, "Antinomianism" rears its head in the church. This is understandable since Christianity in many a "successful" church today has degenerated into a self-help club with an all but exclusive focus on the "political use" of the law (inner-worldly guide). However, the false impression is given that genuine faith could coexist with an unwillingness to fight sin. Baptism's cross of lifelong struggle against sin is rejected.

10. Read 1 Corinthians 10:1–15. Does being baptized and enjoying the Lord's Supper coexist peacefully with engaging in idolatry and sexual immorality? In other words, what is the freedom from sin the Gospel offers *not*? (See also Galatians 5:13; 1 Peter 2:16; and compare to Luke 9:23–24.)

11. Read 1 Corinthians 10:13. Why is this promise so important in the battle against sin?

Spiritual Exercises

- In the coming week, review or commit to memory what Luther's Small Catechism teaches on Baptism.
- This week, read Romans 6:1–4 each day:

  What shall we say then? Are we to continue in sin that grace may abound? By no means! How can we who died to sin still live in it? Do you not know that all of us who have been baptized into Christ Jesus were baptized into His death? We were buried therefore with Him by baptism into death, in order that, just as Christ was raised from the dead by the glory of the Father, we too might walk in newness of life.

- When failing in your battle against sin, comfort yourself by reminding yourself: I am baptized! And then rejoice in Christ's salvation given you in your Baptism once for all.

Point to Remember

We know that our old self ["old Adam"] was crucified with Him in order that the body of sin might be brought to nothing, so that we would no longer be enslaved to sin. (Romans 6:6)

To prepare for "Cross and Sacrifice," read Romans 12:1–2.

C8

Cross and Sacrifice

*The sacrifices of God are a broken spirit; a broken and contrite
heart, O God, you will not despise.*

—King David, *Psalm 51:17*

Christ's suffering and death, His cross, is the all-availing sacrifice for the sins of the whole world. Christ's cross is also every Christian's example for self-sacrificial living according to God's will—in the context of his or her vocations. As seen in the last session, the baptized live by the cross in this twofold way. Saved by Christ's sacrifice, we are called to offer sacrifices, ultimately ourselves and all that we have, to our Savior.

12. What are some examples of personal sacrifice? That you have made for others? That others have made for you?

God's Sacrifice and Our Sacrifices

13. Read Revelation 13:8b (NKJV or NIV); Genesis 3:15; Isaiah 53:5–7; Hebrews 10:1–14; Matthew 16:21; and Luke 24:25–27. From these verses, can Christ's suffering and sacrifice be considered an unfortunate accident of human history? Why or why not?

14. Read Acts 14:22; and 2 Timothy 3:12. As Christ, so the Christian. Why is this so? Read also John 15:19.

15. Read John 16:33; and 1 Peter 4:12–16. What is our comfort in suffering?

16. Read Hebrews 13:15–16; and 1 Peter 2:18–21; 3:14–18. Where do we meet God's will besides the Ten Commandments? In what sense can we then say that we are sacrificing to God when we suffer patiently?

17. Read Galatians 5:22–23. Does it make sense to call this kind of suffering a form of "passive love"? Why or why not?

18. Read 1 Peter 2:5. What makes this (and any) sacrifice to God pleasing in His sight (see also Galatians 5:6)?

Thy Will Be Done

We live in a democratic culture that values very highly personal independence, individual freedom, self-realization, and self-determination. Anything that restricts these "rights" is often looked upon very critically. We want to be in charge of our lives from cradle to casket. However, in the Third Petition of the Lord's Prayer, Christians pray to their heavenly Father that His will, not ours, be done.

In outward Christendom, society's love of freedom expresses itself in the teaching that man is free to "choose" to follow Jesus. When carefully examined, we realize that this is a claim that we are able to emancipate ourselves from the kingdom of the devil and join the kingdom of God, as if both were human organizations or clubs. If we accept this thinking for argument's sake, we might wonder: If our will is stronger than the devil, what prevents it from creating for ourselves a pain-free paradise on earth? The simple answer is: God's will does. He resists the proud.

19. Read John 3:5–6; and Ephesians 2:1–3. What role does human will play in conversion? How does this reflect the Christian's attitude toward suffering sent by God's will? Based on Christ's example as a form of God's will, what is the Christian's "right" in this life (see Isaiah 53:7; 1 Peter 2:23)?

20. In an early sermon on the Third Petition of the Lord's Prayer, Luther asserted that it is good when our will (or our planning) does not come to pass. Comment on this also in light of James 4:13–15. Is there a "Gospel side" to viewing hardships as ordained by God?

Patient Suffering as "Spiritual Worship"

Most people worship some kind of supreme being or spiritual force. Many are very dedicated, sincere, and even intense in their worship life. They, literally, take great pains to make sacrifices of one kind or another to please or appease the god(s) of their religion. For example, some people pray for hours or go on dangerous, costly pilgrimages. Some Christians spend significant sums of money to buy the latest spiritual self-improvement material that promises a successful marriage or career or a victorious Christian life.

Such is the strenuous and impressive worship practiced by the religions of the world. These are governed by the Law written in the human heart by the Creator. Yet Christian worship, at its core, does not consist of doing this or that great feat in honor of the Christian God. At its heart, Christian worship is not *giving* to God (love) but *receiving* from God (faith) what He gives for Christ's sake through the Gospel in Word and Sacraments. The Gospel of Jesus Christ, not a set of religious and moral laws, is at the heart of our lives as Christians. Worship "in spirit and truth" is primarily the passivity of faith in the Gospel, not the ensuing activity of love. We are *declared* righteous; we don't justify ourselves.

21. Passive faith is the "highest worship" (*Concordia:* Apology V 33). By way of analogy, does it make sense to consider patiently bearing God's will (e.g., in a nursing home) a very high form of love? How does this help us to understand Luther's teaching that "temptation" (done *to* us) and not actively helping our neighbor (done *by* us), is the all-important touchstone in the school of the theologian?

22. In view of this high praise for "passive faith" and "passive love," are they good and saving in and by themselves?

Spiritual Exercises

- What hardships are you currently experiencing in your life? Begin to view your hardships, the ones due to no fault of your own, as ordained by God's will and rejoice in being counted worthy to offer such a high sacrifice to God.
- Meditate on the hymn "What God Ordains Is Always Good" (*LSB* 760; *ELH* 519; *CW* 429; *LW* 422; *LBW* 446; *TLH* 521) during this week. How does this hymn point you in the midst of suffering to God's sure promises found in His Word?
- Pray that God would open your eyes and your heart to the suffering of someone you know and that He would give you the courage and resources to provide help and comfort to him or her. Begin now as God's royal priest (1 Peter 2:9) to petition the Lord in prayer on his or her behalf.

Point to Remember

I appeal to you therefore, brothers, by the mercies of God, to present your bodies as a living sacrifice, holy and acceptable to God, which is your spiritual worship. (Romans 12:1)

To prepare for "Temptations and Other Afflictions," read Matthew 4:1–11.

છ

Temptations and Other Afflictions

Consider that according to Scripture it is not at all difficult to be
converted, but to remain in a converted state, that is difficult.

—C. F. W. Walther, *The Proper Distinction of Law and Gospel*

As baptized Christians, we know that we will suffer in our vocations in one way or another. However, we do not know what or when we will suffer. This uncertainty, no doubt, is at the core of attempts to impose certain hardships on ourselves, as if we could thereby "bribe" God to keep the "real thing" away from us. We fear we might not be able to withstand when tempted.

However, for the baptized members of the body of our crucified yet risen Lord, there is no need for bargaining with God or for fear. Instead, every day we confidently commend ourselves, our bodies and souls, and all things to His hands. In the end, all believers shall rise to life everlasting just as Christ is risen from the dead.

23. What associations come to your mind when you think of the word *temptation*?

God's Baptized Children Are Tempted

24. Read Matthew 4:1. The first word of this verse is *then*. To which event in the earthly life of Christ does this little word refer? Why was Jesus led into the desert?

25. According to Matthew 4, how often was Jesus tempted? With what was He tempted? What does this reveal about the state of the Person of Christ at this point in His life?

26. Twice Satan introduces his tempting words by saying "If you are the Son of God . . ." (Matthew 4:3, 6). On what other occasion are these words spoken (see Matthew 27:40)? What do both incidents have in common? In other words, why is Jesus tempted? What does this mean for you?

27. Read Matthew 16:21–23. How was Peter's suggestion a "temptation" for Christ? How did Peter understand what "God's Son" means (see Matthew 16:16)? Was suffering part of it? If Peter had been right, how would the life of the Christian look? Considering that Christians are both saints and sinners, to whom would Peter's original vision be more "attractive"?

28. Satan can quote Scripture quite well. According to Matthew 4, how does Jesus beat back Satan? What does that mean for you (see Genesis 3:1–6; Ephesians 6:16–18)?

29. Christ's last temptation in the wilderness has to do with the First Commandment. How does that impact every temptation you face as a Christian?

Various Origins of Temptations

Satan certainly is an important tempter. But he is by no means the only source of temptations. In his Large Catechism exposition of the Sixth Petition of the Lord's Prayer, "and lead us not into temptation," Martin Luther distinguishes temptations of the flesh, the world, and the devil. He even goes so far as to correlate various stages and vocations in life to temptations of the flesh (the young), the world (the old), and the devil (all who deal with God's Word).

30. Read Matthew 13:3–8, 18–23. What "sources" of temptations are presented here? How does this compare to Matthew 4?

31. Read Matthew 13:18–23 again. Who's to blame for a lack of fruit? What does that mean for overcoming temptations from various sources?

The Resurrection of the Body
and Embracing or Avoiding Affliction

Affliction hurts. It's that simple. That is why human nature tends to avoid suffering and pain. Affliction seems unnatural because it truly is. In the beginning, there was no hardship on earth. However, Scripture teaches us that afflictions are now part of our natural lives in body and soul—we are not in Paradise anymore (Genesis 3). Afflictions are also part of our lives as Christians—we are not yet in heaven (Romans 8). In this life, we cannot avoid pain.

To be sure, Scripture does not advocate suffering for its own sake or encourage people to seek out suffering. In fact, when the Early Church was persecuted in the Roman Empire, the pastors of the Church discouraged Christians from actively seeking martyrdom. Yet they also did not shrink back from unavoidable suffering in the context of their vocations. A pleasant life in this world, tempting as it may be, is not a primary goal for those who have the hope of bodily resurrection.

32. Read 1 Corinthians 15:12–13, 19–24, 30–32; and 2 Corinthians 1:8–9. How did faith in the resurrection of the body strengthen Paul in his earthly trials and afflictions? How was his faith in the resurrection fostered by trials?

33. Read Philippians 1:21–26; and 2 Timothy 2:10. How can these verses help you decide when to embrace and when to avoid suffering in your vocations?

Spiritual Exercises

- This week, meditate on Luther's explanation to the Sixth Petition in the Small Catechism. Notice how we pray for God's strength and help in our battle against "the devil, the world, and our sinful nature."
- Study the hymn "I Walk in Danger All the Way" (*LSB* 716; *ELH* 252; *CW* 431; *LW* 391; *TLH* 413). Reflect especially on stanza five, which points us to the wounds of Christ as our "hiding place" from Satan's power.
- Ponder Luther's Table of Duties in the Small Catechism, confessing your responsibility for the suffering you have caused yourself and others. Trust in God's promise of forgiveness (1 John 1:8–9) and in the comfort God gives us in the midst of our suffering (2 Corinthians 1:3–7) through our Savior, Jesus Christ.

Point to Remember

But in fact Christ has been raised from the dead, the firstfruits of those who have fallen asleep. (1 Corinthians 15:20)

To prepare for "Our Cross with God," read 1 Corinthians 2:1–16.

ᙉ

Our Cross with God

Truly, you are a God who hides yourself, O God of Israel,
the Savior.

—The prophet Isaiah, *Isaiah 45:15*

Our various crosses—our battle against sin, disease, our lack of success at work or in our shrinking congregation—make it difficult to believe in our gracious God. God's mercy and grace often are hidden in our lives. We wish God would reveal Himself clearly and deliver us (or at least get us "over the hump") so that we could "see and believe." We might also long to be vindicated before others who tease or simply ignore us because of Christ and His Word: "See, I was right after all."

However, God does not usually reveal Himself in this way. We do not have any promise to see God with our physical eyes before Christ's glorious return on the Last Day to judge the living and the dead. What we do have, though, is His Gospel. Christ hides Himself under Word and Sacrament to comfort you as you follow Him by bearing your cross.

34. Have you ever felt frustrated with God? How? If you feel comfortable, take some time now to share your experience with other participants.

Hidden from the Eye, Revealed to Faith

35. Read Romans 1:18–25. Why is God hidden from people? What are the consequences of man's failure?

19

36. Read Romans 1:25; 1 Corinthians 2:7–8, 14; and Philippians 2:6–8. Why did "the world" miss the fact that the man, Jesus, is God?

37. Read 1 Corinthians 1:21–24; 2:1–10. What is God's method of bringing them to sight? Is there any preparation to make people more "receptive" to God's Word? Why does God's Word succeed?

38. Read 1 Corinthians 1:17–21, 28–2:5; 3:4–7. Why does God employ such a "foolish" strategy to save the lost?

39. Read Matthew 26:26; and Titus 3:4–7. When looking at Communion's bread and wine and at Baptism's water—what do they miss who say these elements are *mere* bread, wine, and water? Read Mark 2:5–7 and John 20:21–23. When they hear a man forgive sins, many Christians are offended today. What are they missing?

40. What do the means of grace (the Gospel; Absolution; Baptism; and the Lord's Supper) have in common with the humiliation of Christ culminating on the cross? What do they have in common with your suffering in your body?

Hidden to Remain Hidden

As Christ's divine nature on earth was hidden in His human nature, so the glorified Christ is now hidden under Law and Gospel, Word and Sacraments. This is for our good. In the means of grace, we can be certain that we will encounter our crucified and risen Savior with His gifts, even under the cross when we don't "feel" redeemed. At the same time, we are not consumed by the superabundant glory that is Christ's.

However, our triune God is present everywhere, not just in the means of grace. In fact, we encounter Him everywhere, at times for our good, as in the bounty of creation; at times in a damaging, killing way, as in the little and big disasters of this life and world. God is there, in His unsearchable, divine wisdom. He even upholds that creature of His who fell and has since caused many others to perish: the devil himself. Especially in the catastrophes of this life, God has hidden Himself even more deeply. Here we meet God where He does not want to be found.

41. Unexpected good or evil in our lives make us wonder if we have had an encounter with the hidden God. If you wish, share one such encounter of yours.

42. Read Romans 11:33–36; Deuteronomy 29:29; and Matthew 5:3–12. We cannot avoid the hidden God. We can try to explain Him away or deny Him, but He is still there. How does Christ deal with the hidden God? In other words, what might be God's purpose in making you experience Him apart from the Gospel?

The Hidden Church

Christians suffer because we are baptized into Christ's suffering and death. Like our Savior, we are no more than strangers in this world. This is true for us individually; it is also true for Christ's Church on earth. The Church is not a place where we enjoy outward peace and harmony. In fact, the harshest conflicts of all arise in the Church. For here, the truth of God's indivisible Word, and with it eternal damnation and eternal salvation, is at stake.

In his 1539 treatise *On the Councils and the Church*, Luther counts cross-bearing as one of the marks of the true Church, that is, the Church which teaches God's Word in all its truth and purity and uses

21

Christ's Sacraments (Baptism and Communion) rightly. The true Church is the Church hidden under the cross. Luther also notes that churches that take greater liberties when it comes to God's Word and Sacraments often prosper.

43. Read Deuteronomy 13:3; 1 Kings 19:14; Jeremiah 6:14; and 1 Corinthians 11:19. What are the temptations we're dealing with in the Church?

44. Read Matthew 16:13–19; 28:19–20; Luke 12:29–32; and 1 John 4:1–6. How do these passages comfort the Church under the cross? When will we be vindicated (see Romans 8:19; 1 Timothy 3:16)?

Spiritual Exercises

- Resolve to arrive early for worship and to spend time in quiet reflection and prayer before and during the Divine Service (suggested Prayers for Worship are provided in the front flyleaf of *Lutheran Service Book* and other hymnals).
- In addition to cards and flowers, the next time you visit someone in the hospital, take a Bible and a hymnal along and use them to comfort someone laboring under the cross.
- Meditate on the hymn, "Thee We Adore, O Hidden Savior" (*LSB* 640; *LBW* 199). Contemplate the rich imagery of Christ providing us "living food" by giving us His body and His blood in the Sacrament.

Point to Remember

For since, in the wisdom of God, the world did not know God through wisdom, it pleased God through the folly of what we preach to save those who believe. (1 Corinthians 1:21)

To prepare for "God Tempts No One?" read Genesis 22:1–19.

CB

God Tests, the Devil Tempts

Thus the sailor at last still clings
To the cliff which was to destroy him.

—Torquato Tasso (J. W. v. Goethe), *author's translation*

"God tempts no one." This is what Luther's Small Catechism, based on God's Word (James 1:13), teaches. However, there are several passages in Scripture that speak about God testing His holy people, either individually or as a group. Are there then two types of testing, one being done by the devil, the world, and our sinful flesh (temptation); the other being done by God? Are they different and, if so, how can we tell them apart? And, if God tests us, where can we flee for refuge?

45. Do you think it is mean of God to test His children? Why or why not?

"God tested Abraham . . ."

46. Read Genesis 17:19; 21:12. We might raise moral objections to God's command to Abraham to kill his promised son (Genesis 22:2); yet they are raised neither here nor elsewhere in Scripture. In what sense is God's command a testing of Abraham?

47. Read Genesis 22:5, 12; Romans 4:20–21; and Hebrews 11:17–19. What was Abraham's comfort and strength in this trial? What did God's test reveal?

48. Read Genesis 22:8, 13–14. What event on the mountain gives us a glimpse of things to come in Christ?

49. Read Genesis 22:15–18. Does this text suggest that we are saved by "passing God's tests"?

50. Read Genesis 15:3–6; Romans 8:32; and 2 Corinthians 1:20. Before we believe all of God's Word to us, even when it seems to us to be self-contradictory, what do we first of all need to know? What is the major distinction in God's Word?

51. Read Galatians 4:22–31. What does it mean that all who believe in Christ, "like Isaac, are children of promise"?

God's Purpose in Testing His Saints

Why does God test His saints? The scriptural answer is simply this: in order to bring out what is in our hearts. It's not that God would not know this; we need to know ourselves. Tests sent by God thus function like a mirror or, as we might also say, as the Law. They show us what's inside of us. By nature, inside of us is a simple logic: the good get rewarded; the bad get punished. This is the logic of the Law, implanted in man's heart from creation. It is the foundation of our society; it is also the foundation of all world religions.

Many churches and books advertise Christianity as the best world religion, that is, the most reliable way to achieve worldly success and influence. As you've noticed by now, genuine Christianity is different. It teaches from God's Word that things don't work out in this life precisely because we're saved and strive follow the crucified Christ in all things. It is a tremendous comfort to know under our crosses that holiness or success is ultimately unimportant because our salvation does not depend on either our holiness or on our success in life. We're free from the law. Childlike trust in Christ alone makes a Christian, not possessing more or less of His blessings in this life, which include being holier than others. We're free from the Law.

God's tests can take the form of abundant blessing of a material or spiritual nature: an abundant harvest, a long-awaited child (Abraham and Sarah!), even progress in conquering sin or adding new members to our congregation. If we were all spirit, such blessings would posit no challenge for us; we would receive them as what they are: undeserved gifts of our heavenly Father for Christ's sake; they would not get in the way between us and God. God could withhold them anytime and we'd still love and fear and trust in Him only for the sake of the Gospel's gift of eternal salvation. Abraham, at least in Genesis 22, was free from sinful attachment to the gifts of God: He loved Isaac, but he feared the Lord. In the freedom that comes with faith, Abraham was ready to give up this precious gift for a time at the Giver's command, trusting that God would raise him again even from ashes, if need be.

52. Read Genesis 16:1–3; 17:15–19. Abraham at first boldly believed God's unreasonable, laughable promise concerning an heir (see Romans 4:16–19). Why did he waver later in view of this test? What does this reveal about Abraham? What does it reveal about the nature of faith?

53. Read Deuteronomy 8:2–4, 10–16; Proverbs 30:8–9; Psalm 73:1–14; and Matthew 15:18–19. How are we tested, and what does it reveal? What is Satan's purpose in tempting Job (see Job 1:9–11)? How does this, then, clarify the meaning of James 1:13–15 and help distinguish God's testing from Satan's temptations?

"Lead us not into Temptation"—Temptation and Prayer

Our Lord Jesus Christ has taught His Christians to pray: "Lead us not into temptation." Based on what we've seen above, we are *not* asking that God shouldn't tempt us (the petition does not read "Tempt us not"). Part and parcel of God's will for us Christians is to be under the cross in order to rely more and more on the unchanging Gospel in Word and Sacraments, not on the perishing goods of this world, including our strength.

In the abovementioned petition, we rather pray that God would protect us lest we be deceived and misled away from the Gospel "into false belief, despair, and other great shame and vice." The "deceivers" are not just on the outside; we can't blame it all on "the devil." He still has a powerful ally in us, our sinful nature. It, too, contributes its powerful and confusing seductions.

54. Read Psalm 50:15 and Zechariah 12:10 (NKJV). Cross-bearing, including resisting multiple temptations, is hard work for our faith. We will start "huffing and puffing." Where do Christians catch their breath from serving God and neighbor, including for prayer?

55. In a difficult situation, some people might say: "Now all we can do is pray." Do you agree or disagree? Discuss your answer with other participants.

Spiritual Exercises

- When tested by God, turn to the Gospel and prayer.
- When tempted by the devil, turn to the Gospel and prayer.
- Meditate on the hymn "When in the Hour of Deepest Need" (*LSB* 615; *ELH* 257; *CW* 413; *LW* 428; *TLH* 522). Spend time each day this week laying all your woes (stanza 4) before God in prayer.

Point to Remember

God is faithful, and He will not let you be tempted beyond your ability, but with the temptation He will also provide the way of escape, that you may be able to endure it. (1 Corinthians 10:13)

To prepare for "The Purpose of Our Cross," read Romans 8:15–30.

CB

The Purpose of Our Cross

Christ will crown the cross-bearers.

—Johann Sebastian Bach, *an inscription written beneath*
Canon BWV 1077, author's translation

Today, as ever, suffering and hardship are usually regarded as pointless. Certainly, we may believe that hardship builds character. But too much suffering seems to do the opposite; suffering for a while is good and beneficial, but there are limits. In other words, experience teaches us that suffering is not to be desired. The cross, in whatever shape God might send it, hurts. But in the shadow of the cross, the light of the Gospel shines brightly. As Luther put it, in afflictions we will realize how sweet the Gospel really is and become better theologians for it.

56. Why do you suppose it is so difficult to accept that God is in control—especially when we are suffering?

The Image of His Son

57. Read Genesis 1:26–27; 5:3; Colossians 3:10; and Ephesians 4:24. What does "image of God" mean in Holy Scripture?

58. Read Romans 8:15–17; and Galatians 3:25–27. When and how was the image of God, lost in the fall, restored in us, that is, when were we adopted as God's sons?

59. Read Romans 8:28–29. Is the "image of His Son" different from the "image of God"? How does your suffering serve to shape Christ's image in you (see also Romans 5:1–11; 2 Corinthians 1:8–9)?

60. Read Romans 8:19–27. Why do Christians, along with all of God's creation, suffer (see Genesis 3:16–19; Romans 5:12)? How do continuous hardships shape your prayer life? What is most important to remember under these circumstances?

61. Read Hebrews 12:4–12. According to these verses, what is the purpose of affliction? How is this related to being transformed in Christ's image (see Hebrews 12:1–3)? How is God's Fatherly "chastising" different from His "punishing" (see Psalm 32:1–5; 119:67, 71)? How is "being left in peace" by God actually His most terrible punishment (see Psalm 73:12–20; 1 Corinthians 11:27–32)?

62. Read Acts 5:41; 1 Corinthians 1:27–31; 2 Corinthians 12:9–10; and 1 Peter 4:12–13. If we had lost everything in this world but our Savior, could we still rejoice, even boast? Why or why not? How does this relate to Christ's image (see Matthew 4:4; 1 Peter 2:20–21)?

Refreshment under the Cross: Baptism and the Lord's Supper

Baptism holds the sure promise of suffering and cross-bearing with Christ. This promise is inseparably tied up with the promise conveying Christ's cross-earned forgiveness to you. This, however, is

29

not yet the full picture and comfort Baptism indeed offers. For Baptism also conveys God's sure promise that, as we've suffered here with Jesus, we will also live with Him in heavenly glory. So long as we live, Baptism's promise is there for us.

Baptism is by no means the only comforting "rod and staff" God provides for those traveling through life's dark valleys. The promises concerning our forgiveness in Christ, as we read them in Scripture and as they sound forth in the Divine Service, are very important too. The greatest comfort, though, is given in the Lord's Supper. Here not only the promise of forgiveness is applied individually; here the seemingly lonely wanderer has the assurance that he or she is not alone sealed to him or her by Christ's very own body and blood. This is a saving foretaste of the endless marriage feast of the Lamb, while in this life the "cup of salvation" is tied to the cup first drunk by Jesus on the cross. Further, we enjoy earthly fellowship with other believers with whom we commune.

63. Read Romans 6:5; Ephesians 2:4–7; Matthew 16:21, 25; Mark 10:38–39; Romans 8:15–18; and 1 Peter 4:13. How do Baptism's gifts of death and rising relate to our life as Christians? How has Christ's suffering hallowed all our suffering?

64. Read Matthew 26:26–29; Mark 10:38–39; Luke 13:28–30; 22:28–30; 24:39–43; and Revelation 7:16; 19:6–9. A wedding supper in heaven awaits us after sharing Christ's cups of pain and salvation here on earth in faith. What does eating and drinking in heaven say about our resurrected life there?

Comfort under the Cross: Predestination

At times, God's saints undergo extreme trials. If such calamity strikes us, we might fear to "lose faith" and forsake our Savior. God's Word contains great comfort for you in this troublesome situation. First, it teaches that faith is not the same as (frail) human willpower or optimism. Faith is wrought and sustained exclusively by God the Holy Spirit by means of the Gospel in Word and Sacraments. Christian faith is faith in Christ as our one Savior from all sin, death, and the devil. Further, God's Word teaches that Christians are recognized by bearing their crosses patiently as they follow their crucified Lord; suffering is thus not a sign of being forsaken by God.

Then there is Scripture's wonderful teaching on predestination or eternal election. This doctrine confirms that we are saved by God's grace alone, apart from anything in us (including happiness and prosperity). It teaches that, before the world was even made, God chose to save us in Christ. He did so because of Christ's life and death and through the Gospel in Word and Sacraments. We will be saved indeed, even through many tribulations. We know that we are God's elect children by faith in the Gospel of Jesus Christ. Through the means of grace, God provides the strength we need to hold onto Christ by faith.

65. Read Romans 8:28–30; Ephesians 1:3–12; and 2 Thessalonians 2:13–14. What is included in the doctrine of predestination? How does this comfort you under the cross?

66. Read 2 Peter 1:5–10. How can actual steadfastness and faithfulness to God in affliction afford additional comfort under the cross?

Spiritual Exercises

• Spend time each day this week studying and meditating on the following passages of Scripture, which teach your eternal predestination to salvation by faith in Christ's Gospel:

S.   Romans 8:18–25
M.   Romans 8:26–30
T.   Romans 8:31–36
W.   Romans 8:37–39
T.   2 Peter 1:3–11

F.   Ephesians 1:3–9

S.   Ephesians 1:11–14

- Meditate on the hymn "If God Himself Be for Me" (*LSB* 724; *ELH* 517; *CW* 419; *LW* 407; *LBW* 454; *TLH* 528). Rejoice in the warm and bright confidence you have in the "sun that cheers [your] spirit" (stanza 10), Jesus Christ.

- Listen to the St. Matthew Passion by J. S. Bach and hear how text and music work together beautifully to move us from being deeply saddened by our readiness to run away from the cross with Christ's disciples, to being truly relieved from this sin by Christ's willingness to bear His cross for us, to being again eager and ready to receive our cross out of the hands of our crucified Lord.

Point to Remember

For those whom He foreknew He also predestined to be conformed to the image of His Son, in order that He might be the first-born among many brothers. (Romans 8:29)

Leader Guide

Leaders, please note the different abilities of your class members. Some will easily find the many passages listed in this study. Others will struggle to find even the "easy" passages. To help everyone participate, team up members of the class. For example, if a question asks you to look up several passages, assign one passage to one group, the second to another, and so forth. Divide up the work! Let participants present the different answers they discover.

Each topic is divided into four easy-to-use sections.

Focus: key concepts that will be discovered.

Inform: guides the participants into Scripture to uncover truth concerning a doctrine.

Connect: enables participants to apply that which is learned in Scripture to their lives and provide them an opportunity to formulate and articulate a defense of a key doctrine.

Vision: provides participants with practical suggestions for extending the theme of the lesson out of the classroom and into the world.

Cross Meets Man: Baptism

Objectives

By the power of the Holy Spirit working through God's Word, participants will (1) come to appreciate Baptism as one of God's means of salvation; (2) begin to see Baptism's pattern for Christian living under the cross; (3) begin to be able to articulate the correct understanding of Baptism when asked by others.

Opening Worship

O God, for our redemption You have given Your only-begotten Son to the death of the cross, and by His glorious resurrection You have delivered us from the power of our enemy. Therefore, grant that all our sin may be drowned through daily repentance and that day by day a new man may arise to live before You in righteousness and purity forever; through Jesus Christ, Your Son, our Lord, who lives and reigns with You and the Holy Spirit, one God, now and forever.

Sing "'Come, Follow Me,' the Savior Spake" (*LSB* 688; *ELH* 422; *CW* 453; *LW* 379; *LBW* 455; *TLH* 421).

(Focus)

1. Answers may vary. Some participants may not have any conscious connection to their Baptism at all and might simply consider it as a rite that's traditionally performed when a child is born to church members. Others will be able to identify it as one of God's means of grace, that is, those instruments He has chosen to convey the forgiveness, life, and salvation won by Christ on the cross. Some, in reference to the fourth question on Baptism in Luther's *Small Catechism*, may be able to point to Baptism's relevance as we struggle against sin daily by God's Law and Gospel.

Baptism and the Cross (Inform)

2. Paul raises the rhetorical question of whether Christians should continue to sin. In verse two, he will clearly answer in the negative.

3. Baptism unites us with Christ, in both His death and His resurrection. Continuing to sin is out of the question for members of Christ's body. Of course, each of us sins daily. What Paul means here, however, is that the baptized believer should not continue in unrepentant sin.

4. Our crucifixion with Christ happens in a twofold manner: first by faith in the promise of the Gospel presented in Baptism—this is instantaneous—and then by love, that is, by struggling against sin by the power of the Holy Spirit. This second is obviously an ongoing process that will not be completed in this life on earth. Christ, now living in us through faith, is also shaping our thoughts, words, and deeds. He is both saving gift and guiding example.

5. Our crucifixion takes place in our daily vocations as we strive to serve God and neighbor according to God's holy will, the Ten Commandments. Our "members" are to become in life what we are already by faith: God's instruments, God's slaves of righteousness. This is what it means to live by the Spirit and not according to sinful flesh. The fact that we are no longer "under law but under grace" (Romans 6:14) means that we've passed from condemnation to pardon through faith in the Gospel. Obviously, however, this is no justification for willful sin. We continue to sin (which is why we need to strive against it), but sin is no longer the dominating force in our life; the Holy Spirit is.

6. The Ten Commandments clearly give us a picture of our new life in Christ. Their abiding truth for the Christian is expressed in the Small Catechism. The Ten Commandments must not be replaced by a vaguely defined notion of "love" or "what would Jesus do." Love is the summary of the Ten Commandments, not its substitute. In His perfectly obedient life, Christ fulfilled the Ten Commandments for us to liberate us from the curse of the Law. However, Christ's fulfillment of the Law does not mean we should not now strive with the Holy Spirit's help to follow His example. This includes Jesus' cross-bearing. Faith does not replace love; faith makes true love happen. The life we will enjoy in the new heaven and the new earth will be

the full expression of the Ten Commandments; there we will be in life and body what we are now by divine imputation: perfectly righ-teous.

7. Sin is forgiven, but our sinful nature is not removed by Baptism. The "old Adam" (original sin) remains a potent force in us, always bringing forth actual sins and seeking to gain the upper hand. If that were to happen, we would again enjoy sinning; we would no longer sin "against our will." Our will, renewed by the Spirit, now delights in God's holy Law, even under burdens, and is grieved by our ongoing sinning (we are also comforted by the Gospel's full and free forgiveness). This ongoing struggle and defeat (we do not do what we truly want and what God truly wants) is a cross because it is spiritually draining. If it were not for a constant flow of Gospel power through the means of grace, our faith would be completely exhausted. Many churches today reject Scripture's clear teaching on original sin; obviously, they will take a different view on the hardships of the Christian and his or her struggle against sin. For these people, the enemies of the Christian (the devil, the world, and our sinful flesh) are a bit farther removed, so the means of grace are less important or even dispensable. The less sin is emphasized, the less the Gospel is perceived to be needed.

A Closer Look at Baptism (Connect)

8. We are not saved, not even in part, based on our improvement in our battle against sin. We are saved by God's grace through faith in Christ alone, not by faith and love. Faith in the Gospel will show itself in our fight against sin. We will, by God's grace, make progress in this battle. While this is an indication of Christ dwelling in us through faith, under the close scrutiny of the Law this progress will appear insignificant, especially when considering original sin.

9. Churches that do not teach the biblical doctrine of Holy Baptism deprive their people of the comfort that comes with the knowledge of what God gives in and through Holy Baptism. Under the fire of the Law, salvation will become doubtful as well: Did I really believe sincerely or have enough faith when I stepped forward to be baptized (if I did, why do I doubt now)? At times, the teaching of eternal security (once saved, always saved) is adduced to compensate for an incorrect understanding of Baptism. But here, too, confidence is put in "my faith" (back then) not "my Savior" (right now). Another typical compensation is to point to one's emotions, success, or happi-

ness in life as indicators of being saved. This is a purely Law-based assurance (God as justly rewarding the good). This legalism and false assurance of salvation will break down under the trials and afflictions of the cross, as experience (and repeated Baptisms) clearly shows.

On the other hand, the Roman Catholic understanding of Baptism's removal of original sin does not adequately address the continuing power of the sinful nature in the life of the Christian, nor the continuing benefit of and need for Baptism. Other sacraments, especially the sacrament of penance, are said to continue where Baptism presumably has left off. However, the Scriptures point to Baptism, and the promises God attaches to this Sacrament, as of great value not only in our continuing struggle against sin, but also in our sure confidence of our salvation.

Anti-Antinomianism (Vision)

10. Hearing and believing the Gospel and receiving the Sacraments in faith does not jibe with remaining in unrepentant sin. God's saving gifts are not static; they are living gifts that cannot be separated from Christ and His Spirit, the "Lord and Giver of Life." Freedom from sin is the freedom from God's just condemnation for sin on account of Christ. But it is not a license to sin. Part of self-denial, bearing our cross, is also to deny our sinful natures the opportunity to rule over us.

11. At times we will struggle with great temptations to sin. We're tempted to just give in and say: "I can't handle that! Why not give in just this one time? I can always repent later!" This is not a Christian approach. We don't sin in view of God's forgiveness. The promise in 1 Corinthians 10 teaches us to commend ourselves to God, to look to His Gospel for strength to fight sin, and to look to Him for a way out of temptation. God has set a limit for every temptation.

Cross and Sacrifice

Objectives

By the power of the Holy Spirit working through God's Word, participants will (1) become familiar with the biblical understanding of sacrifice that rightly distinguishes Law and Gospel; (2) apply this to a humanistic understanding of freedom prevalent in our culture and in many churches today; and (3) view their suffering as a sacrifice that is pleasing to their heavenly Father for the sake of Jesus Christ's all-availing sacrifice.

Opening Worship

Almighty and everlasting God the Father, who sent Your Son to take our nature upon Him and to suffer death on the cross that all humankind should follow the example of His great humility, mercifully grant that we may both follow the example of our Savior, Jesus Christ, in His patience and also have our portion in His resurrection; through Jesus Christ, our Lord, who lives and reigns with You and the Holy Spirit, one God, now and forever.

Sing "What God Ordains Is Always Good" (*LSB* 760; *CW* 429; *LW* 422; *LBW* 446; *TLH* 521).

(Focus)

12. Answers may vary. Some might think of a soldier leaving a family and career behind to serve his or her country. Others might think of mothers giving up their careers to raise their children, or of fathers doing the same to teach their children "as the head of the household." Others may offer the example of parents saving money to afford a college education for their kids. But also note the opposite: sometimes people selfishly sacrifice everything to "make it big" in life. Clearly, what we choose to sacrifice, and for whom, indicates who or what is most important to us.

God's Sacrifice and Our Sacrifices (Inform)

13. Christ's sacrifice on the cross was not an accident of human history. It was planned by God even before the foundation of the world; there was divine necessity behind it. The Son of God freely pledged Himself to die for sinful humankind even before humankind existed or had fallen into sin. His suffering and death was revealed by way of a promise (Genesis 3:15). It was proclaimed by God's prophets and recorded in God's written Word. It was foreshadowed by the sacrificial rites of the Old Testament. It was fulfilled by Christ during His earthly life, death, and resurrection.

14. As Christ had to suffer, so, too, must Christians suffer. The fallen world cannot peacefully coexist with Christ's members, as it couldn't coexist in peace with Christ. The world's alienation from God expresses itself in hostility toward God, God's Son, God's messengers (prophets, apostles, pastors), and God's people. They are strangers in this world. Christ has called His disciples out of this world, the kingdom of darkness, into His kingdom of light.

15. The Christian's comfort is that Christ has overcome the world. We will have tribulation in this world and suffer many things, simply because we honor God's name by teaching His Word rightly and live our lives according to it. Just as Christ suffered and was glorified, so we, as members of His body, will suffer and be glorified. Suffering as a Christian does not drive the Spirit away; it is therefore not a sign of God's wrath! Like Christ, we suffer because we are God's children. We can "rejoice in our sufferings" (Romans 5:3; see also Colossians 1:24; 1 Peter 4:13), because we know that we are joined to Christ.

16. We meet God's will in this world also as it allots us hardships and suffering in the context of our vocations. His revealed Law in the Scriptures is our guide. Enduring these God-given sufferings is a form of doing good, following Christ's example. It is therefore a form in which we, in response to Christ's sacrifice, sacrifice ourselves and all that we have. Suffering justly, for example, as an impenitent criminal, is no such sacrificing. Christian sacrifices are not sacrifices to gain or merit forgiveness; they are sacrifices out of thanksgiving and praise for the forgiveness given in the Gospel for Christ's sake and received through faith.

17. The gift of the Holy Spirit through the Gospel brings forth all sorts of good fruits, patience being one of them. Elsewhere (Galatians

5:6), Paul teaches that faith is active in love; "love" is thus the summary of faith's fruits brought about by the Holy Spirit. In Romans 13:10, Paul summarizes all of God's will in love. Patience in suffering is therefore a form of loving God. Since patience is not "active" in the narrow sense of the word, we can call it "passive love."

18. No matter how impressive a human sacrifice is (including severe suffering), it is not pleasing to God unless it is offered in faith in Christ. This is to say, it is only pleasing to God when it is offered without the sinful intention of appeasing God through it. This intention is only "put to death" by faith in the Gospel, that is, by trusting that we are at peace with God for the sake of Christ's once-and-for-all sacrifice in His life and death on the cross.

Thy Will Be Done (Connect)

19. While our love toward our neighbor is *active,* our will in conversion is *passive.* Hence, Christ uses the analogy of birth. We don't conceive ourselves, nor do we contribute to our conception in any shape or form. Rather, we *are* conceived. We don't give birth to ourselves; we *are* birthed by our mothers. In suffering, we likewise are to remain passive. Think of yourself as a patient in a hospital, where you depend on others to feed, wash, clothe, and medicate you. That's not an easy thing to do; being active and productive all the time is what we are taught. Suffering, especially when we're in a situation where we can't free or help ourselves, reminds us that God takes care of us even without our active involvement. He does so even when we sleep; He also brings us, dead in trespasses and sins, to life by the Gospel. When we see Christ as the patient Lamb of God who commends Himself to Him who judges justly and does not take matters into His hands, we see that the Christian's "right" and privilege is to suffer with Jesus. A life of "soft clothing" (Matthew 11:8) is not that of a disciple of Christ who follows his or her Savior in the context of his or her vocations. "Human rights," which for some now include the right to have an abortion, to marry someone of the same sex, and to experiment on human embryos, reflect *humanism,* not Christianity. Christians following their servant Lord focus on serving their Creator and their fellow creatures, not on serving themselves.

20. Luther clearly understood from God's Word that our sinful flesh goes against God's will. It does not desire God's will, but rather hates and rejects it at every turn. By not letting our sinful desires

come to fruition, God is guiding us to conform to His will, to let go of our ideas and to adopt His. In our blindness, we at times think that we are the lords of our lives. Yet a sudden turn in fate shows us that we are not in charge and that, compared to God's might, our plans are nothing. This is a humbling experience of God's will (Law). The sinner in us will obviously forever rebel against God's will—he or she wants to have it his or her way. Yet the Christian in us does indeed pray and wish: "Thy will be done." God is not an obscure force of nature that plays dice with our lives. For us, God is the loving, wise Father. His will, whatever He may ordain, is best, even though we first may simply believe this based on the Gospel. And when hardships don't come from some anonymous fate, then we can pray to our gracious God and Father who gave them to us, trusting that He knows us well and means well for us.

Patient Suffering as "Spiritual Worship" (Vision)

21. Indeed, it makes sense to place patient cross-bearing way up on the list, because it is so closely reflective of the role of faith in justification: purely passive and receptive, receiving the good things God gives. Suffering also belongs to those things God gives through which He works for our good. We don't have the blessings of the cross won by Christ without the painful experiences of the cross in our own lives (see Matthew 10:37–39; Luke 9:23; 14:27; LC I 42; FC SD XI 49). We receive both passively. Usually, "active" Christians are held up as our great examples and, usually, their activities aren't really part of their vocations. An "exemplary Christian" is the Christian athlete pointing to heaven or saying a prayer who is lauded for his or her "faith." In contrast, the suffering of a wife as she takes care of her infirm husband, or the patient, invisible suffering of parents at the hand of a wayward child, or the perseverance of the widow in the nursing home or hospital—these things often don't appear on our radar screen. They don't seem to be very important; after all, so the thinking goes, nothing is being "done."

However, great things are happening here. Christians, by God's grace, are "doing" patience. Obviously, when it comes to doing things, we at times have greater control; but when it comes to enduring God-sent, not self-chosen, suffering, that control is not there. We have to resign ourselves fully to this special gift of God. This makes suffering and temptation the "touchstone" that will reveal whether our faith is genuine or whether we serve God only for the sake of material advantages.

22. Obviously, apart from Christ neither faith nor love saves us. Love doesn't save us because we're saved through faith in Christ alone. And faith, by itself, doesn't save us either. That might be surprising, but faith doesn't save us because believing is such a great deed or character trait that God rewards. Rather, faith must have an object. Faith in Christ saves because of what it receives, namely, Christ and His saving benefits. Love is the Gospel-motivated response of the believer, accomplishing the good works that God has prepared for us beforehand (Ephesians 2:10). This includes patience under the cross.

Temptations and Other Afflictions

Objectives

By the power of the Holy Spirit working through God's Word, participants will (1) recognize that temptation and suffering come in various forms; (2) discern the aim of Satan's temptations; and, (3) in light of the hope of the resurrection of the body and in the context of their vocations, begin to discern which afflictions to embrace and which to avoid.

Opening Worship

O almighty and eternal God, we implore You to direct, sanctify, and govern our hearts and bodies in the ways of Your laws and the works of Your commandments that, through Your mighty protection, both now and ever, we may be preserved in body and in soul; through our Lord Jesus Christ, Your Son, who lives and reigns with You and the Holy Spirit, one God, now and forever.

Sing "I Walk in Danger All the Way" (*LSB* 716; *ELH* 252; *CW* 431; *LW* 391; *TLH* 413).

(Focus)

23. Answers will vary here. In our culture, perhaps, the most common associations with the word *temptation* seem to have to do with sexual desires and food. However, the devil, the world, and our sinful flesh tempt us in every aspect of our lives.

God's Baptized Children Are Tempted (Inform)

24. In this passage, the word *then* (Greek: *tote)* refers to the preceding narrative about Christ's Baptism in the Jordan River by John the Baptist. There, the Son of Man, the Son of Mary, was revealed to be God's own Son. Following His Baptism, Jesus was led into the

desert by the Holy Spirit in order to be tempted by the devil and to successfully defeat him through using God's Word.

25. Jesus is tempted three times based on His hunger, His physical vulnerability, and His weakness in worldly terms—all of these three are aspects of His humiliation. That is to say, they're based on the fact that, after the incarnation, which included the immediate communication of all divine attributes from the Son of God to the Man, Jesus, the Son of God "made Himself nothing," concealing His glorious form of God in the meekness and humility of human flesh. He only rarely used or displayed His divine attributes, never for His own good, but only to heal and save others. Christ's humiliation, which made these temptations by the devil possible, was the necessary presupposition for His work as Savior: only the Son of Man in His humiliation could be obedient to His Father and die on the cross (see Galatians 4:4; Ephesians 2:14; Philippians 2:6–8; Hebrews 2:14–18).

26. Jesus was tempted by those same words again when He was hanging on the cross. In each instance, Christ was tempted to lay His humble state aside and show His divine glory fully. If He had done this, His work of salvation would have become impossible, as stated above. Satan might also tempt you by playing your high spiritual status (child of God) against your humble life here on earth, where you serve your neighbor hidden away in some office building or farm or family kitchen: "Don't you deserve better? How about 'the best life now'?" Being God's children is by such opinions clearly equated with the absence of suffering and hardships, displaying victory and success, and everything revolving around our needs. Christ is different. He was and is all about serving, not being served (Mathew 20:28). He's not an upgraded man; He's our gracious God who stoops down in human flesh to serve us. We should likewise serve God and our neighbor humbly according to God's unchanging commandments, even under our crosses.

27. Peter, like the devil and the folks at the cross in Jerusalem, has a "natural" understanding of what a god is, does, and how he should fare on earth (if he ever cared to come down). God does not suffer. So, if Christ is this god's son, he ought not to suffer either. As those who follow such a god without pain, we'd be also entitled to a life of glory and privilege, eventually conquering our every challenge. Obviously, such a vision of Christianity would be very pleasing to our sinful nature, our "flesh and blood," which might want to follow Je-

sus but only if there's no price to be paid, no sacrifice to be made along the way.

28. Jesus defeats Satan with God's Word. Jesus certainly gives us also an example of how to deal with a tempter: Use the "sword of the Spirit" lest you be deceived by the devil as Eve was in Paradise. There's no "higher power" we can appeal to—God's almighty Word is it, and it will be sufficient. To use this sword skillfully, we obviously need to practice swordsmanship, that is, we have to learn this Word well and apply it to our life and experience, always rightly distinguishing between Law and Gospel. This kind of learning begins at home; it is reinforced at church and out in the world.

29. In all temptations, the First Commandment is at stake, because the First Commandment, as the Small Catechism shows, is the backbone of all the other commandments. If we do not look to Christ, the Second Person of the Trinity, for all good things in this life and the next, then all other steadfastness and discipline will be of no avail. But the opposite is also true: we cannot claim to be believers in Christ when we readily give in to temptations to sin as they are presented to us—as if those temptations had a greater power or importance than the one true God.

Various Origins of Temptations (Connect)

30. We can indeed summarize the sources of temptation as Luther did: the devil (snatches the Word out of man's heart); the sinful nature (is too shallow to allow the Word to take roots that weather the scorching heat of persecution for the faith's sake); and the world (has so many cares, or interesting things, to lay on our weak shoulders that the Word becomes an afterthought). In a sense, Matthew 13 applies Matthew 4 to us: Jesus didn't have a sinful nature that would resonate with the world. So there was just the essential conflict of Satan versus God. As far as we're concerned, there are a couple more players in the field (flesh and world), but the ultimate battle is still between God and the devil. Giving in to self and world is always giving in to the devil. There is no neutral ground.

31. Obviously, we ourselves are to blame if the Word doesn't take root in us. This means that the power to overcome temptation can only come from outside of us, from God's Word itself. We are to blame for unbelief; God is honored for our faith and perseverance.

The Resurrection of the Body
and Embracing or Avoiding Affliction (Vision)

32. Faith in the resurrection of the body afforded Paul an imperishable hope that lies beyond this world of death and decay, of changes and chances. It mightily comforted him in his trials, which at times might have seemed endless, certainly too much for his weak powers. The resurrection Gospel reminds us that afflictions are not endless. God has set an end for them. Trials on earth make faith in the resurrection more precious; a miserable life makes a life without misery very desirable. In this way, Paul's faith in the resurrection was fostered, while this faith, as all Christian faith, is created by the Spirit through the Gospel. This, in a sense, is a Law/Gospel relationship: the Law shows us our sins, which makes the Gospel of forgiveness precious; hardships in this life make "the life of the world to come," and the promises concerning that life, very precious.

33. Paul had to endure many hardships in life due to his vocation as an apostle of Jesus Christ. (He did not go around idly volunteering his services and then get into trouble; Paul did what God had called him to do.) Therefore, the trouble that comes with our vocations in church, home, work, and state we have to endure for the sake of our neighbor. We do endure them in the certain hope that they, too, will not be endless. We therefore need not end them prematurely, as if a life of hardship is not a life worthy of God's children. But we also need not take the "whole world" and its misery on our shoulders. That is God's work (John 1:29). He's the adult here; we're but the children. For us, He has cut the world into little pieces for us in our vocations, which are overwhelming sometimes. When we fail in our vocations, the Law will drive us to the Gospel. We can thus remain human creatures; we don't have to becomes gods, not even when it comes to "helping" others.

Our Cross with God

Objectives

By the power of the Holy Spirit working through God's Word, participants will (1) begin to appreciate more fully God working through Word and Sacraments; (2) begin to understand the concept of hidden versus revealed God; and (3) begin to appreciate the hidden, oppressed nature of the true Church of God on earth.

Opening Worship

Almighty God, gracious Lord, pour out Your Holy Spirit on Your faithful people. Keep them steadfast in Your grace and truth, protect and comfort them in all temptations, defend them against all enemies of Your Word, and bestow on the Church Your saving peace; through Jesus Christ, Your Son, our Lord, who lives and reigns with You and the Holy Spirit, one God, now and forever.

Sing "A Mighty Fortress Is Our God" (*LSB* 656; *ELH* 250/251; *CW* 200/201; *LW* 297/298; *LBW* 228/229; *TLH* 262).

(Focus)

34. Answers may vary. We can be very frustrated with God sometimes. Not only does He, for our good, prevent our plans from coming to pass, but also He hides Himself. This is obviously painful when His hiding means that we suffer persecution for Christ's name (Matthew 5:11).

Hidden from the Eye, Revealed to Faith (Inform)

35. God's power and divine nature can be perceived in what is created. However, due to sin, people fail to worship God as God and instead worship fellow creatures (extraordinary animals and people)—and declare this to be supreme wisdom! In other words, special gifts given by the Creator (such as intelligence) are used to justify the worship of creatures. By turning away from worship of the Creator to

the worship of creatures, people turn in on themselves. The result of this breaking of the First Commandment is God's wrath and moral confusion imposed by God as punishment. At the same time, some knowledge of God and morality is left even among unbelievers because God's Law, "hard-wired" into us, has not completely been erased by sin. The various non-Christian religions bear witness to this. They make man's inner-worldly efforts and achievements the basis of salvation; they only know the Law (and that imperfectly), but not the Gospel. They worship idols, not the one true God: Father, Son, and Holy Spirit.

36. In Jesus Christ, the Creator humbled Himself by becoming a creature. Even though the world engages in creation-worship, it missed the Creator in human flesh because it expects great power and majesty. Instead of standing out as Creator by His stature or power, Jesus hid Himself in flesh and blood in order to be subject to God's wrath on the cross.

37. God opens blind eyes through the "unreasonable" message of a crucified God and Savior, which, in worldly terms, is offensive. God cannot suffer and be weak, let alone die as a criminal; only humans can, and only sinners deserve it. This message does not make sense to man's fallen, Law-bound reason, just as Jesus of Nazareth as God doesn't make sense. This is why the Gospel *is and remains* a mystery, not the fact that it's not known as a piece of information. Both incarnation and crucifixion are indeed foolishness to the natural man, that is, the unbeliever. There are no exceptions. People cannot be prepared for God's Word by human activities. It is God's Law leading to a realization of one's sin and God's wrath over sin that prepares hearts for the Gospel, which creates faith when and where it pleases God. The Word of God in Law and Gospel succeeds where it succeeds because the Holy Spirit is present in it and at work through it. Suffering can prepare the unbeliever for God's Word in the same sense a speeding ticket can: both suggest to us that we are neither immortal nor almighty. But both experiences have limits, as encounters with God's Law hidden in creation, and need the clarifying word of God's revealed Law to be driven home, that is, to work genuine repentance by showing the full extent of sin's damage in man (original sin). The Gospel "makes sense" only to the person who has recognized his or her utterly lost state before God and who has been given the supernatural gift of faith by the Holy Spirit through the Gospel.

38. God uses worldly folly because worldly wisdom has proved truly foolish by not recognizing Him. In this way, God punishes and destroys disobedient wisdom and makes all people equal. We're not saved based on our IQ, since no IQ of the world can know the mind of God. So we can't boast in what's in us, in certain creaturely gifts that we have; we can only boast in the Lord. The foolishness of the message works like the Law in that it humbles the proud and prepares them for the true wisdom of God. This holds true both for speakers and hearers of this message. When someone is converted, it is not because of some special gift in the speaker or in the hearer in addition to the Word itself.

39. Some obviously miss the divine power that is in these elements of bread, wine, and water by virtue of God's Word being added to them. They judge based on reason, that is, what they can experience by their senses or cogitate in their minds. The same holds true for a pastor, on the basis of his office as God's servant, forgiving sins. This, too, is done based on God's power in His Word, which is added to the human voice since Christ instituted Absolution after His resurrection. Also, through "mutual conversation and consolation" (SC III IV), believers extend God's gracious Word of forgiveness for Christ's sake to each other.

40. The means of grace are very humble instruments of God's service among us to forgive us our sins. This makes them, like Christ's humiliation, easy targets for ridicule. Some Christian churches practice Baptism and Communion; they preach. But they teach that these God-commanded rites or activities are mere human activities. They do not believe God's Word, which teaches that God *does* give His saving grace in Baptism and Holy Communion as Christ instituted them, and in the Gospel purely proclaimed, read, shared, or remembered. These Christians believe that the power has to be added to it from the outside, either on the part of the hearer or of the speaker. This makes sense to fallen reason—after all, some believe, others don't; some are "effective" preachers (like Billy Graham, Joel Osteen, Rick Warren), others aren't. But this only leads to boasting in human qualities and qualifications; it doesn't give glory to God who has chosen to save through a foolish Word preached by foolish men (1 Corinthians 4:10). Jesus was rejected often—does that mean He wasn't God in those instances? People are converted when and where it pleases God, but they're always converted by means of God's Word. As the means of grace don't look like God's chosen instru-

ments, as Christ in His humiliation didn't look like God's Son, so we, too, will not look like God's children in this life. Suffering and hardships, but also sin, will hide our true identity for the time being. But that doesn't mean we aren't God's children when we suffer! Rather, we can humbly wear our sufferings as badges of honor.

Hidden to Remain Hidden (Connect)

41. Answers may vary. On the positive side, which is often not acknowledged because it is less "traumatic," we might see a bumper crop or a promotion or a healing against all odds. On the negative side, there might be the death of a child or seemingly endless trials and afflictions, but also unusual cruelty, for example, German concentration camps in World War II, the Stalinist Gulag, or the terrorist attacks of 9/11. How can God permit these things to happen? Why does He keep alive the perpetrators of these crimes?

42. We're called to leave the hidden things hidden. We should not try to figure them out. There might not be a satisfying answer in God's Word to every question that is raised by hardship and cross-bearing. Jesus directs us to turn our eyes away from what we cannot fathom to the blessings that are ours by faith in the Gospel, even in the midst of tantalizing why-questions. Our many unanswered questions concerning God in this world might go unanswered—but God in Jesus Christ is there in the Gospel.

The Hidden Church (Vision)

43. Hard questions for Christians are questions like: Why is there disunity in outward Christendom? Why do people not embrace the Gospel of salvation more willingly? Why is the full truth of the Gospel often persecuted and denied most vigorously in the Church? A short answer to all these questions is, of course, that this is so because of sin. But, then, why doesn't God prevent sin from having these effects in the church? One answer given by Scripture is that we see here a test of God to reveal to us what is in our hearts, whether genuine faith or unbelief posing as faith. If there are false teachers who teach their views in God's name—they might, for example, preach only the Gospel without calling people first to repentance, as did the false prophets in the days of Jeremiah—then we are called to avoid them. Yet it just makes more sense to go along with the majority, not with the truth of God's Word; to walk by sight, not by faith.

In other words, even in the Church, a realm often portrayed as one of harmony, the cross awaits us. Jesus, too, was rejected most fiercely by the religious leaders of the time. We now live in the Church militant; the Church triumphant in heaven is yet to come.

44. False teachers are popular because they speak nothing that is fundamentally opposed to the world, even when (or especially when) strict moral demands are made. The Law is no mystery to the world; the Gospel is. And yet, the true Church does have God's solemn promises that it will not be conquered by all the hordes of Satan. Even this "little flock" is not without a helper, because the one true God, Jesus Christ, is its Shepherd, not from a distance, but presently governing His flock in and through His Word and Sacraments in the hands of His ministers, the pastors. These promises, not statistical charts, are our comfort under the cross in the Church until we are vindicated on the Last Day, when we will rise to life everlasting in heaven with all believers in Christ who have fought valiantly the good fight of faith on earth.

God Tests, the Devil Tempts

Objectives

By the power of the Holy Spirit working through God's Word, participants will (1) become acquainted with the biblical teaching that God tests His saints; (2) begin to see the purpose of God in testing His saints; and (3) begin to understand how we can pray to God under the heavy burdens of our particular cross.

Opening Worship

Almighty God, because You know that we of ourselves have no strength, keep us both outwardly and inwardly that we may be defended from all adversities that may happen to the body and from all evil thoughts that may assault and hurt the soul; through Jesus Christ, Your Son, our Lord, who lives and reigns with You and the Holy Spirit, one God, now and forever.

Sing "When in the Hour of Deepest Need" (*LSB* 615; *ELH* 257; *CW* 413; *LW* 428; *TLH* 522).

(Focus)

45. Answers may vary. Some might think yes, others no. Reasons given may vary. Some might feel that this makes God kind of unpredictable (testing = playing tricks). Others, better versed in Scripture, might assert that being tested by God is beneficial for better self-knowledge.

"God tested Abraham . . ." (Inform)

46. God's command for Abraham to slay his own son seems to go against His promise to Abraham concerning the promised offspring from Isaac. It also seems to undo the promise already fulfilled concerning Isaac himself.

47. The promise of the resurrection of the dead comforted and strengthened Abraham for the horrible task before him. The trial re-

vealed that Abraham clung to God's promise by faith; he "feared the Lord," even above his beloved son. This faith made Abraham confident that he and the boy would return to the servants waiting at the bottom of the mountain. He did not worship Isaac as his idol, even though he loved him as his son.

48. God's provision of a substitutionary ram on the mountain pointed forward in time to His own Substitute, the Lamb of God, God's own Son, which the heavenly Father would sacrifice for the sins of the world. On His cross, Jesus took our place and suffered God's wrath for us. The God-Man became our substitute. Being Abraham's beloved son, Isaac also foreshadowed Jesus, the Father's beloved Son.

49. Abraham is certainly commended for his obedience by the Lord's angel. But consider that he was already declared righteous in Genesis 15:6 through faith in God's promise. In all this, he remained sinful by nature, as his failures to believe in God show (see question 52 below), and therefore unable to save himself. His astounding feat of obedience on the mountain was a direct fruit of his saving faith. However, in addition to his eternal salvation (which is by faith in the coming Messiah), God grants Abraham the great privilege of being the ancestor of that Messiah through whom the entire world would be blessed, that is, delivered from the curse of the Law (see Galatians 3:13–16).

50. We first need to believe in the Gospel, the good news concerning Christ our Savior from all sin, death, and the devil; in Christ all the promises are yes and amen. The major distinction in God's Word is the distinction between Law and Gospel: the former promises certain death to the sinner; the latter promises life and salvation for Christ's sake. By the Holy Spirit's work through the Word, we "believe the Law," that is, accept its death sentence over us due to our sin and "believe the Gospel," that is, accept God's judgment of "not guilty" because of the life, death, and resurrection of Jesus Christ. Compared to believing both the Law *and* the Gospel as God's Word, the rest of Scripture is, really, fairly easy to believe. And yet, faith in Scripture's teaching is always wrought by the Holy Spirit, not brought about by us, since we're here not dealing with mere factual information (for example, about how the world was made and how long it took), but with how these facts are related to our salvation in Christ.

51. As "children of promise," we are the spiritual children of Abraham, related to him by way of faith in the same promise concerning the Messiah. Isaac, while being Abraham's biological child, was first conceived after the promise was made. He was, as Paul says, "born through promise," just like we are begotten by the promise that our sins are forgiven, we're free from the curse of the law, and God's abundant blessing is ours for the sake of our substitutionary Lamb, Jesus (Galatians 3:16, 26–29). Like Isaac, we have to endure persecution from unbelievers. Flesh and spirit cannot be at peace, neither within (Galatians 5:17) nor without (Galatians 4:29). And we're always tempted to complete in the flesh what we've begun by the Spirit—we'll always be tempted to slide back under the Law and make our salvation dependent on something we do or have in addition to what Christ has done, be that our prayers, our faith, our devotion, our suffering, or our success in life.

God's Purpose in Testing His Saints (Connect)

52. Abraham later wavered because he looked away from God's promise to his own problems and solutions to them. This quickly ate up his faith so that he took matters into his own hands to fulfill the promise concerning a son. This shows that Abraham wasn't "by nature" a trusting person, any more than you and I are today. Abraham was a sinner like us, who, by nature, doubted and rejected God's Word and promise. He, too, was more impressed by God's gifts than by what he heard from God in His Word. Faith lives on God's Word of promise, which will sound particularly joyful, albeit unrealistic, in trials. If we tune our ears away from the promises God makes in His Word, we're sunk.

53. We are indeed being tested, as the Israelites were when they were led into a desert hostile to life, by being led into hardships where we don't see anything good except God's promise—will we then cling to God and His promise, or doubt and rebel? Will we be envious of the prosperity of the wicked? Testing also happens when we're richly blessed, financially or otherwise—these blessings can become either our "just rewards" we think we deserve because we're such great Christians or our idols (more important than God) without which we don't want to live when God takes them back. God's purpose in testing is therefore to lead us to know our hearts; to save us

from spiritual arrogance; and to lead us to the unchanging Gospel, there to strengthen or renew our faith.

Satan's temptations, on the other hand, seek to lead us away from the Gospel, by leading us either into carnal security or despair. Carnal security means that we're led, not to repentance, but to believe that our sinning doesn't matter, since "God loves everybody just the way they are." Despair means that we're led to believe, not that our sins are forgiven by God for Christ's sake, but that our sins are too serious to be forgiven—and that our difficult, humble life indicates that we're forsaken by God for good (Satan's temptations of Job thus continue by means of his legalistic friends!). Satan's temptations therefore confuse Law and Gospel, while God properly applies the Law's mirror to lead sinners to the Gospel. God cannot lie or deceive; even when He tests us He works for our eternal salvation.

"Lead Us Not into Temptation"—Temptation and Prayer (Vision)

54. We "catch our breath" in the Gospel, and from the Gospel alone. There the Holy Spirit breathes new life into our hearts; we then breathe out that same Spirit in prayer to our Father through His Son, Jesus Christ.

55. Some might agree, others disagree, and both can be correct! It all depends on properly distinguishing Law and Gospel. The statement is wrong if it is meant to say that, if we only pray sincerely or hard enough, God will change His mind because of our earnest prayers—as if prayer could force God's hand. However, the statement is correct if it is meant as an expression of our faith that resigns itself fully to the good and gracious will of our heavenly Father. In the former case, it would be an expression of human activism that seeks to control even God; it would be born out of unbelief. In the latter case, it would be an expression of faith's passivity that looks to God's gracious activity and will for all good things.

The Purpose of Our Cross

Objectives

By the power of the Holy Spirit working through God's Word, participants will (1) know what the image of God/of the Son means; (2) come to realize that this image is formed, not deformed, in them through suffering; and (3) come to rejoice in the gifts of the Gospel, given in Word and Sacrament and confirmed in the doctrine of predestination.

Opening Worship

Merciful Father, since You have given Your only Son as the sacrifice for our sin, also give us grace to receive with thanksgiving the fruits of His redeeming work and daily follow in His way; through Your Son, Jesus Christ, who lives and reigns with You and the Holy Spirit, one God, now and forever.

Sing "If God Himself Be for Me" (*LSB* 724; *ELH* 517; *CW* 419; *LW* 407; *LBW* 454; *TLH* 528).

(Focus)

56. Opinions may vary. Some might reject any thought of bad and evil in connection to God. More mature individuals will know that God works good through bad all the time—He kills by the Law to make alive by the Gospel.

The Image of His Son (Inform)

57. In Scripture, "the image of God" means that man "looked like" God spiritually, not physically. Therefore, Adam and Eve, being created in God's image, knew God and His will perfectly and lived accordingly in relationship to Him and His creation. Theirs was "original righteousness," they did God's will with ease, "by nature." After the fall, this image was lost. Original righteousness and natural

integrity were lost and replaced by original sin and natural corruption. God's image was replaced by Adam's image.

58. God's image, lost in the fall, is restored in us through Baptism when original sin is not removed, but forgiven along with all other sins. This is when we are adopted as sons of God. The image is first restored by way of imputation. God declares us righteous and holy for Christ's sake. Through faith in him, all knowledge and wisdom of God is ours. In the new heaven and the new earth, the image of God will be restored in full actuality and life, the corruption of original sin having been removed at death or on the Last Day.

59. The image of the Son is not different from the image of God. The Son *is* God. Suffering helps it to take shape in that it trains us in Christlike patience and perseverance. In other words, what is imputed to us by faith is to shape our life as well. By faith in Christ, we are perfectly patient under our crosses already; Christ's perfect patience is credited to us. But our lives now should also become Christlike and patient, though at times this might mean that we will look like the "man of sorrows," beat-up, bloody, and all (Isaiah 53:3; John 19:5), before our bodies will be glorified like His. The power to be patient does not come from our suffering (or from the examples of Christ and His saints); it comes from the Gospel. When faith is exercised in love (including patience, the passive form of love)—and it is *always!*—then there needs to be food for faith, which is the Gospel in Word and Sacraments. Suffering is designed to let us despair of our own powers and seek refuge in God's strength, made available to faith in the Gospel.

60. Christians, in solidarity with all of God's creation, suffer because our first parents, Adam and Eve, fell away from God and brought His deadly curse upon the entire world, including humanity. This curse is done away with by Christ; the blessing comes in the Gospel. Yet this does not take away from the believer the temporal consequences of sin like disease, failing families, and other hardships. These afflictions shape our prayers in that often we will lament and groan to God under the burdens we and fellow creatures bear. It is most important to remember that it is the Spirit who brings our prayers to God's throne; we don't have the power to do that. The Spirit is available only in the Gospel, where it gives us rest from our labors and new breath to cry: "Abba, Father" (Romans 8:15; Galatians 4:6).

61. Hebrews 12 teaches "chastisement" as one purpose of afflictions. By letting us experience some of the temporal consequences of our sins, God reminds us of our sinfulness and sin's fruits. He thereby reminds us of our constant need for His forgiveness and thus keeps us close by the Gospel—when chastised, we should seek God's forgiveness and the strengthening of our faith in the Gospel. Out of our faith thus strengthened will arise the renewed zeal to struggle against sin to please our heavenly Father. Christ's righteousness and obedient endurance is already ours by faith, but our lives now ought to become more like His as well. By reminding us gently (when compared to eternal death in hell) of our ongoing need for forgiveness and by thus leading us to the Gospel, God works a greater outward conformity to Christ in us. God's chastisement is a fruit of God's love; His punishment grows out of His wrath and therefore affects those outside of Christ. Yet it, too, seeks to lead the sinner to the Gospel. It is therefore a terrible punishment of God when He gives impenitent sinners an easy life; how will they ever come to repentance when God seems to reward their wickedness?

62. Yes, we'd still be able to boast, because by faith in Christ we have, in Him, everything, even if we can't feel or see it right now. God's grace is indeed sufficient for us because it forgives us all sin and offers the hope of resurrection and ultimate deliverance from all evil. Christians live by God's Word alone and thereby follow Christ's example. Obviously, what is true by faith in Christ is not yet fully evident in this life. We still do depend on other things, albeit against our will; our faith is weak, it struggles against sinful unbelief. Christ's image still is being shaped in our lives to conform to Him more and more. Suffering aids in this process as it weans us from this perishing world and directs us to God's imperishable Word. The power to benefit from suffering in a godly manner comes from the Gospel alone.

Refreshment under the Cross: Baptism and the Lord's Supper (Connect)

63. As Baptism has connected us to Christ's death and resurrection, we shall also be raised in glory with our head, Jesus Christ. Here we suffer with Christ, in heaven we shall be glorified with Him. Whenever we remember our Baptism, this cooling breeze from eternity gives us new breath in the heat of the battle against sin, tempta-

tion, and despair. Christ describes His own suffering and death as a baptism, a submerging that kills. Our suffering, by God's grace, makes us more patient because it kills off the old Adam (who doesn't like to suffer) until he is finally destroyed in our ultimate suffering, that is, in physical death.

64. When Jesus instituted His Supper, He spoke of the future meal in heaven with those who would believe in Him on earth. He often spoke of our heavenly communion with God in terms of a large banquet. This teaches us something about our life in the new heaven and new earth in that we will have glorified bodies, like Christ's body following His resurrection. Christ himself ate after His resurrection to prove to His disciples that He was not a ghost but their Savior who has not shed His human body. We, too, will have real, resurrected bodies that can eat and drink, even though they won't need food or drink. As a result, when we suffer in the body, when our bodies are disfigured by disease, condition, or accident, we can look forward to that day when our bodies will be made new.

Comfort under the Cross: Predestination (Vision)

65. The doctrine of predestination teaches that God chose us in Christ before the foundation of the world. Furthermore, it includes that this adoption and salvation through Christ takes place in time by means of the Holy Spirit creating faith through the means of grace. For those called according to God's eternal election, all things, even suffering, will work for our eternal salvation as we, according to our callings, lead holy lives. This will of God cannot be frustrated. The elect will be preserved unto eternal life. God will strengthen our faith through the Gospel, and by faith in the Gospel we will also know that we are God's saints who cannot be separated from His love in Christ because we are elected in Christ in eternity to be saved in time through God's Word.

66. Actual steadfastness in trial and under the cross gives evidence of the presence of God's Spirit in us. It therefore affords additional comfort under the cross in that it shows to us that our faith is genuine and not a delusion.

Appendix of Lutheran Teaching

Below you will find examples of how the first Lutherans addressed the issues of cross-bearing and afflictions in the life of the Christian. They will help you understand the Lutheran difference.

We Teach, Believe, and Confess—The Cross

As outlined in the introduction to this Bible study, the cross in the life of the Christian was discussed by the first Lutherans in the sixteenth century. In the Roman Church, self-imposed, self-chosen afflictions had become one of the ways people were taught to cooperate in their salvation. Lutherans rejected the idea that a person could cooperate in his or her salvation (either by actively doing good or by passively suffering evil) because pointing people to their works at this point confuses Law and Gospel: this confusion infringes on what Christ has accomplished by His active and passive obedience and makes man's salvation uncertain ("Have I suffered enough and with the right attitude?").

Augsburg Confession

Paul also says, "I discipline my body and keep it under control" (1 Corinthians 9:27). Here he clearly shows that he was keeping his body under control, not to merit forgiveness of sins by that discipline, but to keep his body in subjection and prepared for spiritual things, for carrying out the duties of his calling. Therefore, we do not condemn fasting in itself [Isaiah 58:3–7], but the traditions that require certain days and certain meats, with peril of conscience, as though such works were a necessary service. (XXVI 37–39)

God's precepts, and God's true service, are hidden when people hear that only monks are in a state of perfection. True Christian perfection is to fear God from the heart, to have great faith, and to trust that for Christ's sake we have a God who has been reconciled [2 Corinthians 5:18–19]. It means to ask for and expect from God His help in all things with confident assurance that we are to live according to our calling in life, being diligent in outward good works, serving in our calling. (XXVII 49)

Apology of the Augsburg Confession

The Ten Commandments require outward civil works, which reason can in some way produce. But they also require other things placed far above reason: truly to fear God, truly to love God, truly to call upon God, truly to be convinced that God hears us, and to expect God's aid in death and in all afflictions. Finally, the Law requires obedience to God, in death and all afflictions, so that we may not run from these commandments or refuse them when God lays them upon us. (IV [II] 8)

The difference between this faith and the righteousness of the Law can be easily discerned. Faith is the divine service (*latreia*) that receives the benefits offered by God. The righteousness of the Law is the divine service (*latreia*) that offers to God our merits. God wants to be worshiped through faith so that we receive from Him those things He promised and offers. . . . For faith justifies and saves, not because it is a worthy work in itself, but only because it receives the promised mercy. (IV [II] 49, 56)

Job is excused though he was not troubled by past evil deeds [Job 2:3–10]. Therefore, troubles are not always punishments or signs of wrath. Indeed, terrified consciences should be taught that there are more important purposes for afflictions [2 Corinthians 12:9], so that they do not think God is rejecting them when they see nothing but God's punishment and anger in troubles. The other more important purposes are to be considered, that is, that God is doing His strange work so that He may be able to do His own work, as Isaiah 28 teaches in a long speech. . . . Therefore, troubles are not always punishments for certain past deeds, but they are God's works, intended for our benefit, and that God's power might be made more apparent in our weakness. (XIIB (VI) 61, 63)

Large Catechism

If we would be Christians, therefore, we must surely expect and count on having the devil with all his angels and the world as our enemies [Matthew 25:41; Revelation 12:9]. They will bring every possible misfortune and grief upon us. For where God's Word is preached, accepted, or believed and produces fruit, there the holy cross cannot be missing [Acts 14:22]. And let no one think that he shall have peace [Matthew 10:34]. He must risk whatever he has upon earth—possessions, honor, house and estate, wife and children, body and life. Now, this hurts our flesh and the old Adam [Ephesians 4:22]. The test is to be steadfast and to suffer with patience [James 5:7–8] in whatever way we are assaulted, and to let go whatever is taken from us [1 Peter 2:20–21]. (III 65–66)

To feel temptation is, therefore, a far different thing from consenting or yielding to it. We must all feel it, although not all in the same way. Some feel it in a greater degree and more severely than others. For example, the young suffer especially from the flesh. Afterward, when they reach middle life and old age, they feel it from the world. But others who are occupied with spiritual matters, that is, strong Christians, feel it from the devil. Such feeling, as long as it is against our will and we would rather be rid of it, can harm no one. For if we did not feel it, it could not be called a temptation. But we consent to it when we give it the reins and do not resist or pray against it. (III 107–108)

The act or ceremony is this: we are sunk under the water, which passes over us, and afterward are drawn out again. These two parts, (a) to be sunk under the water and (b) drawn out again, signify Baptism's power and work. It is nothing other than putting to death the old Adam and affecting the new man's resurrection after that [Romans 6:4–6]. Both of these things must take place in us all our lives. So a truly Christian life is nothing other than a daily Baptism, once begun and ever to be continued. For this must be done without ceasing, that we always keep purging away whatever belongs to the old Adam. . . . This is Baptism's true use among Christians, as signified by baptizing with water. Therefore, where this is not done, the old man is left unbridled. He continually becomes stronger. That is not using Baptism, but working against Baptism. (IV 65, 68)

Glossary

antinomianism. The teaching that the Law has no place in Christian proclamation or in the life of the believer. This view was championed by John Agricola at the time of the Reformation. It was rejected by both Luther and the Lutheran Confessions as it ultimately turned the Gospel into a new law.

cafeterianism. An attempt to create one's own worldview by selecting, cafeteria-style, religious or moral concepts, ideas, and practices from a variety of sources. A person who attends a Christian church on Sunday while believing in reincarnation might be viewed as a "cafeterian," for example, since bodily resurrection and reincarnation are inherently incompatible.

Darwinism. An explanation for the existence and diversity of life on earth, attributed to Charles Darwin, which includes such concepts as evolution, natural selection ("survival of the fittest"), adaptation, and other concepts.

Deus absconditus. The hidden God or God as He hides Himself.

Deus revelatus. The revealed God or God as He reveals Himself in Christ.

efficacy of the Word. The power of God's Word to effect or accomplish its divine purpose.

enthusiasts. A term used by Luther to refer to the radical spiritualists who believed that God came to them apart from the external instruments of Word and Sacrament.

fundamentalism. A movement in the late nineteenth and twentieth centuries that stressed the inspiration and inerrancy of the Bible over Darwinism and other aspects of Enlightenment thought.

Gospel reductionism. Using the Gospel to suggest considerable latitude in faith and life not explicitly detailed in the Gospel.

humanism. A broad range of philosophies that emphasize human dignity and worth and recognize a common morality based on universal, rational human nature. Humanists who deny the possibility of any supernatural involvement in human affairs are sometimes called *secular* humanists.

modernism. A cultural movement emerging in the late 1800s and later emphasizing the inevitability of human achievement (especially through science and technology) and a positive view of human reason, particularly in its ability to determine the truth.

mysticism. While mysticism itself is a broad form of spirituality with distinct nuances, it is best characterized by the movement to transcend or move above the earthly through inward experience.

postmodernism. Refers to a cluster of themes that are somewhat interconnected in their opposition to the attempts to establish truthfulness, which characterized the period of modernity. The focus of postmodernism is characterized by pluralism and the rejection of claims to absolute truth.

oratio, meditatio, tentatio. Prayer, meditation, and trial. Luther said that theologians (students of God's Word) are made by prayer, meditation, and the trial of life under the cross.

rationalism. The Enlightenment movement that saw human reason as the ultimate criterion for reality.

reductionism. A *modern* concept focusing on the human ability to reduce complex ideas or things to simple or more fundamental ideas or things. *Fundamentalism* exhibits reductionism in its attempt to reduce the Christian faith to very few "key" concepts or teachings. *Gospel reductionism* makes a similar error by devaluing or outright rejecting God's Law in the life of the believer (see also *antinomianism).*

revelation. God's act of making His will manifest in both Law and Gospel to human beings. The instruments of God's revelation are the prophetic and apostolic Scriptures.

sola scriptura. Scripture alone. Scripture is the singular fountain of Christian teaching and the final rule by which to evaluate all proclamation in the Church.

sufficiency of Scripture. The Scriptures are sufficient for the purpose that God gave them, namely to impart saving knowledge of Jesus Christ.

Theology of glory. Theology of mystic and scholastic speculation, which holds that true knowledge of God derives from the study of nature, which reflects God's glory. A theology of glory focuses on human reason, mysticism, or morality.

Theology of the cross. A term gleaned from Luther's Heidelberg Disputation of 1518. Theology that is derived from the study of the humiliation, sufferings, and death of Christ.